THE CURED ARNO

6

D1496333

Jack Clemo was born in 1916 near St Austell, Cornwall. Son of a clay-kiln worker, he received only a village school education, but devoted himself entirely to writing throughout a restless adolescence. He remained a mystical recluse during his twenties, living in poverty with his widowed mother. By 1955 he had become deaf and blind.

His first published novel, *Wilding Graft*, won an Atlantic Award in Literature from Birmingham University in 1948. An allegorical novel, *The Shadowed Bed*, which he wrote soon afterwards, was eventually published in 1986 by Lion Publishing. He wrote two volumes of autobiography, *Confession of a Rebel* (1949) and *Marriage of a Rebel* (1980), both recently reissued in paperback by Hodder, and a record of personal faith, *The Invading Gospel* (1958), reissued by Lakeland Books in 1972 and by Marshall and Pickering in 1986.

His first collection of poems, *The Clay Verge*, appeared in 1951, and was incorporated in a larger volume, *The Map of Clay*, ten years later. *The Wintry Priesthood*, a sequence which won an Arts Council Festival of Britain poetry prize in 1951, was also printed in *The Map of Clay*. Four other collections of poetry followed: *Cactus on Carmel* (1967), *The Echoing Tip* (1971), *Broad Autumn* (1975) and *A Different Drummer* (1986). His *Selected Poems* (Bloodaxe Books, 1988) was a Poetry Book Society Recommendation. This was followed by two further collections from Bloodaxe, *Approach to Murano* in 1993, and *The Cured Arno*, published posthumously in 1995. He published two books with Cornish imprints, *The Bouncing Hills*, humorous dialect stories and light verse (Truran Publications, Redruth, 1983), and *Banner Poems*, local descriptive pieces (Cornish Nationalist Publications, 1989). *Clay Cuts*, an illustrated limited edition of early clay-image poems, was published by Previous Parrot Press, Oxford, in 1992.

He was awarded a Civil List pension in 1961, and an honorary D.Litt degree from Exeter University in 1981. He married his wife Ruth in 1968, and in 1984 they left Cornwall to settle in her home town of Weymouth in Dorset. Their courtship and marriage was the subject of a biography, *Clemo: A Love Story* by Sally Magnusson (Lion Publishing, 1986). Jack Clemo died in 1994.

The Cured Arno

JACK CLEMO

BLOODAXE BOOKS

ISBN: 1 85224 326 0

First published 1995 by
Bloodaxe Books Ltd,
P.O. Box 1SN,
Newcastle upon Tyne NE99 1SN.

Bloodaxe Books Ltd acknowledges
the financial assistance of Northern Arts.

Cover printing by J. Thomson Colour Printers Ltd, Glasgow.

Printed in Great Britain by
Cromwell Press Ltd, Broughton Gifford, Melksham, Wiltshire.

For
SARA RAMSDEN
guide and organiser
of the trip to Florence

Publisher's Note

Jack Clemo completed *The Cured Arno* shortly before his death in July 1994. This edition presents the collection in the form in which he wanted it published, but with the addition of a later poem, 'Quenched', at the front of the book. This was written after he visited his old cottage at Goonmarris, near St Austell, with Ruth Clemo in May 1994, when he found the clay works abandoned and the place lightless at night. 'Quenched' was written in the last of the seven Silvine exercise books that contain *The Cured Arno*, but at the back and upside down after many blank pages. A description by John Hurst of the Clemo MSS in Exeter University Library is published in the *Journal of the Institute of Cornish Studies* (autumn 1995).

Contents

PREFATORY NOTE

In this collection of poems, as in *Approach to Murano*, my Italian
visits gave me a symbol that illuminated even those poems which
have no connection with Italy. The cured Arno may represent the
cured ego, and sometimes I only showed the situation that needed
cure. Dante knew his river only in its sick state. It was later "cured"
of its erratic and treacherous behaviour, its destructive winter
floods and the stench of its dry mud bed in summer. The river
image was apt for my purpose, whether I wrote about the *Titanic*
disaster, which cured an earlier generation of its blind trust in
mechanical progress as the key to a safe world, or about my late
marriage which cured my warped and bleak isolationism.

My thanks are due to the editors of the following periodicals in
which most of these poems were printed: *Acumen*, *Christian*, *Cornish
Banner*, *Cornish Guardian*, *Dorset Year Book*, *Symphony* and *The Cut*.
'Growing in Grace' was first published in an appendix to *I Proved
Thee At The Waters*, a booklet written by my mother, Eveline Clemo
(Moorleys, 1976), and later included in *The Oxford Book of Christian
Verse*, edited by Donald Davie (Oxford University Press, 1982).
'Wheal Martyn' appeared in Bill Headdon's anthology, *Cornish
Links* (Kernow Poets Press, 1993).

JACK CLEMO

Quenched

I have returned in fitful spring rain
To the knot of hills that will never untwist
In trick lighting again, as it did while I lived here.
The hill-knot fantasy has been abolished:
Its switches are stiff and unused, ignoring the sunsets.
No current jabs at the clotting shadows
With strange hints of industrial magic.

Tip-flare, pit-spurt, tank-twinkle –
They thrilled me for years, but they have gone.
The hamlet dwellers are dismayed
By the sudden plunge into wartime blackout,
A daily trauma, the final sting
Of failure in trade bargaining.

I'm glad I escaped this blow:
The clay fantasy blazed around my cottage
When I last slept there. I had watched it, drawn
Into a glow of mystery, not costs and markets.
But I avoid the house now:
Its dark night has no message for me.

PART ONE

The Tower

South of the Arno
The cheeky cicadas are shrill,
Catching the zest of perpetual childhood,
Not the aged croak, the irritable warning,
Falsetto quaver from worn-out hearts.
A scan of life as vanity
Could never occur to me here.

I can understand Browning's last whim,
Planning a tower, a Pippa memorial
High on the crest of Asolo,
The town of silkmills, flamboyant melons,
Vines and dusty people.
He had seen some lives changed at a crisis
Through blithe blades of random song.

From his tower he would have gleaned new points
Of sprawled Tuscan splendour, gazed down
Towards the Arno valley, long barred to him,
But still vibrant as he recalled it,
Catching hours of levity
Or consecration in pure moonlight.

He would have foreseen healthy changes:
The unwearied river pushing into Florence,
Corrected and stately, entering the shadow
Of medieval stone visions, holy or grotesque
As lizard and cicada. Either vein would fit
Those ripples now worthy to pass
Giotto's tower, Via Mazzetta
And the trumpeting doors of Casa Guidi.

Delabole Quarry

Carvings on slate in churches
Must be oddly out of key
With the clang in a gaunt crater,
That hacked ragged hole
Where nothing flawed can be mended
Or softened, like clay rock, by a water rinse.

I peered down at the quarry once in childhood
And felt its bald veined ridges
A cold inferno, breathing a foreign climate
More remote from my building mind
Than the weirdest neurotic sculpture.

No basis for art was intended
When a workman sliced his piece,
Curious only to discover
If it were sound for roofing
Or whether the good part looked big enough
To support a decent field gate.

The roofs and posts protected me
While I slept or wandered in Cornwall,
But my art works on warmer material,
And I've never seen a portrait on dull slate.

Voyages

I seemed tagged for steerage travel,
Boarding life while Haig's guns cackled
After the Atlantic warning, the glacial
Stab at complacent luxury.

A dazed world received me, its towering era
Gored hollow – the callow trust
In the perfect engine, the Marconi spell
Welding a listening brotherhood, an evolving race.
Power had been thought infallible
In shipowners, shareholders, blandly claiming:
'Our vessel is unsinkable'.

The lumbering, mindless iceberg
Added an effective footnote:
Even Haig must have sensed an omen
In the dark and off-course
Plunge of the *Titanic*.

I write this eighty years later,
Merely hoping that the ship's string band
Kept enough soul to send the hymn-tune soaring
Above the exploding boiler.

The hymn's truth fixed my class –
Not steerage, below water level,
Sealed from daylight and the nimble deck rain
And the image of a lighthouse
Alert in the moon's broad caress.

No fetid air withered my faith
While slick machinery nagged
Near again and the wrangling tides
Of revived progress rocked the betrayed hull.

Silver Wedding
(for Ruth)

Spiky boughs have borne the soft foam
Of lilac blossoms in a Rodwell garden,
And all Weymouth seems bathed in the flowering
Of delicate vows once spoken
Above dry, spindly growths in a far valley.

We felt no sad advancing shock
Of twinned veins thinned at bedrock
By twisted mirrors of a lost youth,
Girl-bride dazzle of domes and spinning
Dream-cut angles of a honeymoon.

We started cramped in a grey clay gut,
Midlife worn, though with a salvaging trust
In Providence; and, years ahead,
Rich palms appeared, broad white-ribbed beaches,
Enchanting as our destined touch of Venice,
But framing the home gate, the private lilac.

Two tongues of sand are washed near us,
Patches of broken stone submerged,
Adventurous feet barred, as ours were,
From the piercing stabs of a changed surface
First golden-smooth, warm with false promise.
Waves ebb from the sands, but our lapping guard stays high.

Symbol of safe marriage, even for a poet:
These Dorset tides heave with a blind rhythm
That rocked men of word-pouring vision –
Hardy, Hugo, Byron – who were yet
Split, exiled from anniversaries
Of the intact hearth and fountain.

Channel sea-birds may scan our red roof,
Which covers no exile here:
My tongued, modest stream,
Art-tinged, pulses from ribbed fidelity
Unreached by great souls unguarded.

18

Our toast of celebration
Is raised in a winter that feels springlike
With lilac scent in an unsplit harbour.
Our Weymouth sherry slides pure on the lips,
Cresting the mature pledge.

Beatific Vision

Gaunt to the marrow, iron-scarred
As the jail he fled from at Toledo,
The monk John thanked heaven for absolute
Unbroken darkness. A cutting tick of light
Would have betrayed him, and he fancied
An inner parallel.

The soul's disgust with temporal comfort, its taste freed
From festive candles, romantic moon.
John scorned them as carnal flickers
Foiling the escape from self
To the sublime, unrivalled union,
God's clasp of the stripped ascetic.

Did not some wedded Spanish artist
Find a healthier way after baptism
Through the bride's smile, ripe olive-groves in a painting?
He would have known blessed kindlings, the heart's
And high art's vowed frontiers
Heaven-flushed outside the world's prison,
And spirit purged for its last prayer
When farthest from the cloisters.

Lake Paddle

Only a wry parody of pain
Stirs in shod feet that tread lake water,
Stumbling on sharp points of broken stone
Packed loosely near the old Cumbrian mountain.

There's a thrill of escape, immunity.
I took the long cast-out road
To clasp this hand, reach her level:
She who wades with me shared the dry hazard.

It's not an ancient cowled ghost
That could mock me (though the friar landed here),
Nor the sick fall of Ruskin's classic bid:
I had common ground with the normal seeker.

This is a Sabbath immersion.
My memory cannot wince amid fragments
Of promises made here, for it is sheathed,
Wrapped warm to foil the cut, the stab of negation.

We do not deal with tides: the lake shore
Intones no flattery or withdrawal.
Church chimes at Keswick alert our steps;
Cupped ripples laugh under a soaring buzzard.

Kirkstone Pass

High winds slap a remote spine
Hollowed by slate-quarries; the desolation
Peels down to the sullen shiver
Of Brothers Water. Wordsworthian peace
Of Rydal and Grasmere seems a foreign memory.

We enter the ancient inn, sit at a rough board,
Drink coffee that is home-filtered rain
With foreign grains to give it a sweet flavour.

I think of fifteenth-century gales
Buffeting a priest's work – these thick walls
Which screen black beams and good English ale.
He pitied the wayfarers, showed true charity.

Travellers were festive here at Christmas;
Carols challenged the harsh blasts
Pounding from Raven Crag. Coarse life exulted
With a strange foreign flavour barred once from an inn.

Lulworth

(for Catherine Labdon)

No lull in the gusty ferreting
Of Lulworth's secrets while we were there
On that outraged winter morning.
The Dorset gale puffed to its height
To oblige or disturb all objects
That could be pushed or levitated
Or trained in stoic values.

The sea was a thunder of foam, whipped white,
The loose dry sand blown far, stinging my skin;
The whole cove stretched dreary, drained of its hues.
We were the only group in sight
As we battled, gasping a few quips,
From our car to the sturdy inn.

A hesitant lady clutched her walking-stick
And limped unsteadily, needing support,
While a young girl whooped with delight
At the noise, the sense of a rocking world
Not grimly menacing but up to mischief.
She skipped ahead, brown tresses fluttering,
Her clothes a colourful and crazy
Flapping of feminine fabrics in grey air.

She alone braved the open beach
The rest of us were glad to find shelter
In a sociable room, sipping hot coffee.
The storm made me think of wreckage –
Not merely the sucked black hulks in Lulworth bay.

Some poets had come here, choosing a mild day,
But truly shipwrecked. No lull in their denials
Of the high mercy which, at a touch,
Can turn the negative din of fate or fashion.
I sat immune, my life-style's
Praise of heaven amused by the Dorset weather.

Anne Brontë

Timid fawn of the moors, goaded to battle
Against Byronic vice and the soiled lectern.
Microcosm under the Robinsons'
Renowned Victorian facade
A cruel eye-opener.
Just the old intransigent story
Of the uncured self,
The sly and private storm-tracks
Bursting the trained smile.

Gross dregs of the 'Black Bull'
Slinking within the polished tutor,
Even her brother.
Cheap melodrama of moral weakness
Toppling the London promise:
Branwell the brilliant, swaggering painter
Was lost in the burning
Which scattered ashes on parsonage pride.

Anne's own patient governess skill
Proved powerless against her flighty pupil,
Girl-bud brazen for copulation,
Gretna Green farce and the tarnished
Fevers of a faithless actor.
Meek and hymn-writing Anne
Awoke and almost fainted, aghast,
Till she scorched her dainty prayer-book
With venomous insight, utter disgust
At the race that called itself human.

There was irony: she returned to the hymn-scorning
Shelter of the impious Emily,
Stoic, unshocked by evil,
Though this was only another form
Of uncured ego, and disillusion came
Before Branwell died and her defiance
Lay hacked and unbreathing
On the prosaic death-sofa.

Anne's faith revived then; she groped back,
Love-crossed and dying,
To the hint of a remedy
Beyond time, as she had proclaimed it –
A sunny childhood's assured flutter
To the unburst smile.

Anne Brontë became a governess at the home of the genteel Robinsons. One of her pupils disgraced the family by an elopement and a disastrous marriage. Anne's brother Branwell, a tutor in the same household, added further scandal by having a love affair with Mrs Robinson.

Newman

Too stagnant in Bonifacio's
Strait for that rapier mind!
Dead calm had parked a vessel
Some miles from Napoleon's isle, but here,
More bruised than a toppled emperor,
The sick priest paced the deck, watched a distant
Shore-light at night. What light could be kind
Which did not lead him further?

He was led on by a higher gleam,
But always as a sad exile,
A misfit, target of Church storms,
Official bans on his outreach
Souring the Cardinal's splendour.

Strange to us now, his wistful
Trust in the mercy of doubts,
His fear of a breezy passage
Through straits where song and laughter
Showed a faith beyond his austere hope,
Sure of each promised harbour.

Fever Zone

I will not celebrate dead cicadas,
Though many were scorched to cinders, trapped
Down in the puffed Mediterranean foot
While I climbed the breezy hills of Vallombrosa.

Fierce heat ends the grotesque chirps,
So loud and lovable, and as it saps
A human bliss too, I am fulfilled
Without the far south – even Naples harbour
Thinning the lava-trauma of Pompeii.

Some tourists seek a fevered start
To a casual romance – a climate
Unrefreshed by rain but potent in the blood
For the brief leap, the sun-blared freedom.
Well, there are hordes of mosquitoes
Adept at spoiling even honeymoons.

When being enriched by Italy
I stay in its temperate zones
Where cicadas don't get trapped by a long drought.
Their piping would sound healthy, innocent
If it haunted my dreams of her who travels with me:
My fed nerves are not scorched or bitten.

Journey North

A fumbling rail strike started,
Threatening to leave us stranded
Amid costly tombs of Dante, Michelangelo,
Mrs Browning and other visionaries.
The irony was stark and chilling:
Those higher gleams, the artist-prophet's
Notation in verse or stone drew pilgrims
Across a continent to taste the immediacy
Of homage, yet they could be trapped
By a blind dispute about the running of engines.

The Arno pulsed so blue and tranquil
That morning, a hot Sunday, and the breeze
Alerted stuffy corners with joyous bell-peals.
We felt clogged in crisis, but crossed ourselves
At a formal service, knowing we were booked
To have our next sleep near St Mark's,
At a hotel in far-off Venice.

Soon after lunch our luggage bumped
Towards Florence station in a taxi.
One daring train had not joined the strike,
And we caught it. Three hours of wonder
Glowed for us even in the tunnels
That hollowed the dark green Tuscan hills.
Rails had replaced some grapes and olives,
But we thanked heaven for the open way,
Sealing and healing a pilgrim purpose.

Our carriage rocked through the flat northern plains,
And we did not deplore the modernised cities –
Bologna, Padua – where new passengers
Bustled aboard. If these halting-points
Lacked a taintless visionary spell,
We sped on in unshaken sun-blaze
Till the familiar dream-islands glittered
And mundane threats no longer mattered.

PART TWO

Headway

A building at Pisa sagged
Without a bomb-shock, in an age of dark fever,
While Florence was tricked by a waterway
Which artists cursed for its satire,
Flung in deluge or silt
Against their quest for loyal beauty.
The two marred cities grew tense,
Distrustful, and were often at war.

Flitting past Pisa's truant tower,
Monk and harlot alike were fear-gripped,
Awaiting the final tilt,
The snap, the thunder of burial.

But the walls stood leaning for centuries,
And no longer fascinate
Through peril alone: brains grew alert
With engineering skill,
And the tower looks straighter today.

In Florence you feel the depth
Of a trusted rhythm, the hour of repair
Turned timeless. The painter finds his colours,
Fluid reflections, constant for his brush.
Strong patriot's pride is freed
From the drum of a petty tyrant:
No city now plots a raid
On its neighbour, only a valley's breadth distant.

You see the surface advance,
Gifts of cold probing, invention,
Or wiser grounding in politics;
But the heart stays vulnerable, in flux,
Or prone to an off-centre pull.

Stourhead
(for Dilys Ralston)

The only Dorset river
I ever looked at splits near me,
Confused by the row of rooted arches
At Sturminster. I stood there years ago,
Watching the leaf-fingered stream,
But now travel on, thinking of sources.

I have crossed the eastern border
Into Wiltshire, chosen my emblems
From Stourhead rather than Stonehenge:
Lush fertile Grecian bounty,
Guarded and trained while church bells rang,
Not while a Druid's knife dripped blood
Under a weird pillar.

A flight of chaste rock steps dropping down
From the nerve-centres, the ancient house,
The temple of Apollo, sleek, unjarred
By cheap discords; the shy grotto
Suggesting a secret vision;
Broad open lake glassing a clear heaven,
Its ducks peaceful beside the flagstones.

Such grace of art and nature
Troubled me once, a half-pagan shadow,
But, like the distant Arno's change
Through guided manipulation,
The Stour's source yields a hint of healing
Unknown to barren Stonehenge and the brute
Force of a grim ritual.

I am back in Dorset where the Stour spreads,
A humble everyday push of water,
Both where the classic mind
Infused a Greek myth, a Tuscan tang.

At a Devon Abbey

We arrived where an earth tremor had passed
And the stained glass glowed unsplintered;
The busts of abbots loomed cool and cosy,
Unshocked by the temporal lurch.
That moment of aberrant stirring
And threat of the wide snarl
Died less developed than the male chant.

Footsteps are slow and sober in the crafts room
Where monks' hands fashion pregnant trifles:
Common skills, protected
Under flowing habits of sanctity,
Preach survival through modest emblems.

We came away with just a pencil-sharpener,
Shaped like a monk's vest,
And some Benedictine toffee:
Reminders of the invincible signature,
The sweetness of unshaken truth.

George Müller

He would have shocked Devon anyway,
That madcap turned pietist,
God-tracked from his native Saxony.
Before he yielded, reached the Teign
And Keats's shade, there was a kinship
Between wafted poet and plodding, prose-burdened student.

Wand-waving, word-weaving, the pagan spell
Fierce under delicate fancies – these, for Keats,
Bred torment through the inspirer's caution or scorn;
And dry husks, abstract in divinity courses,
Could not guard virtue when thick Prussian blood
Relit carnality near inns and brothels.

Demure, perplexed, the church-folk around Teignmouth
Had stared at Keats a few years earlier,
But Müller prompted a friendlier awe.
This quirky penitent, refusing
Schedule and salary, had captured Shaldon
With a childlike love, a seer's prophetic eye
And a slow tongue groping for English.

He had once been jailed for petty crime
And dead drunk as often as Keats,
Arrogant at Halle and, flushed at cards,
drawn into brute-heat by a haggling kiss.

The London poet seemed a sick moth, fluttering
To his grave in Rome and casting on the Teign,
The Exe, the Shaldon cottages,
The venom of a starved, orphaned dream.

Young Müller soon dreamed of orphans,
Spurred by his Exeter wife, pregnant in Bristol,
And a century of humdrum philanthropy,
Haggling humanism, was struck by a seer's gamble,
Herding his multitudes of children
Outside the well-planned tracks of survival,
In a Bible-fenced corral of stubborn prayer.

The saints' way of emptiness, blind trust in God.
Its vindication is historic:
It bred no melancholy art.

George Müller, a lecherous German student before his conversion, became
the most remarkable Christian philanthropist in Victorian England. He built
and maintained five orphanages at Ashley Down, near Bristol, relying entirely
on faith and prayer, never advertising or appealing for funds.

Ashley Down

Uphill from the Avon, beyond graceful Clifton,
The German Müller raised five towers by faith,
Shielding a horde of urchins. His raw mysticism,
Doggedly Western, no glide of detachment,
Tested eternity with unabashed prayers
For soap and treacle, sacks of potatoes,
Oatmeal, sugar, cans of milk.

He taught ten thousand orphans
To feel heaven's awe in the clatter of breakfast
Where there had been no food, no money
As he pressed his petition an hour before.

Dawn often loomed lean over Bristol,
Threatening starvation for the Ashley waifs,
But Müller smiled on his secret stair,
Having talked to his Chief through the undrugged, timeless
Mediation and heard the brisk whisper:
'The goods are being sent'.
And the vans arrived, mysterious
As freak craft from outer space,
Loaded to forestall the hunger pangs.

In his youth, on a gale-gored Rigi spur,
He had gazed with pagan pride
Across Calvin's majestic province –
Glacier, lake, the refuge city;
But now Genevan signals jabbed
From those Avonside towers – the predestined means
And moments of the divine answer.

Salieri

He bargained with omnipotence:
He would forego the marital bliss,
Be strict and pious if heaven would make him
Creative in art, a great musician.

He fancied that heaven bowed to this:
Time dubbed him Austria's court composer, trilling
Thanks to his obliging deity –
Until he heard Mozart.

Deep in that irreligious clown
Sound-clusters gathered, an unruly fountain
Grew strangely pure, sprayed melodies
Far beyond Salieri's range. The stung ego
Flared, imagined a divine cheat.

Mad hands wrenched a heavy crucifix:
There was great heat, then ashes
And a cold asylum cell.

It's safer to be whimsical
About heaven's irony in the art world's
Gamut of gifts – to enjoy common comforts
While the high bargainers lose all.

George Sand

The geese cackled on at Nohant.
Its imperious lady had ruled her circle
Of eccentric artists and free-lovers
Amid rural peace, pungent air,
The instructive behaviour of animals.

But age brought cancer and a grope for wisdom.
Beyond the farmyard. Her voice crackled,
Pleading with France: 'Kill politics!
Scrap all its rival programmes
That universal love may blossom.
Without brotherhood we're lost, and it's released
By ending the fight for political power.'

This seemed like mad idealism,
But when had she not been mad,
A queen of hearts and dunghills? She wrote books
Which horrified Catholic France, denouncing marriage
As a Papal cage for weak women
Who craved a silly sacrament
Instead of full-blooded joy defying custom.

Her background had not taught her
To build her life free of the bitter sand.
Her parents both had bastards before they wed;
Her husband was unfaithful after scarring
Her genius-sensitive nerves on the bridal night.

A rare, split adolescent,
She flamed into a fury of revolution
That left a mark, though brief, even on Venice
When poet Musset took her there as his mistress.
He sometimes slipped from her at the hotel
And prowled in midnight fever by the canals,
Hunting for a cheap brothel
While his supposed partner planned quick solace
Through another man's caresses.

If she glimpsed an ideal love, it withered
In the heated core of indifference, a cynic's ardour
Wrenched into rage and the clever sting
Which bred a crueller strife and hatred
Than any political tension.

Her pagan conquests have survived
Only as art that scholars wrangle over:
The geese cackle on at Nohant.

Values

(for Gwen Pearce)

Coast road to Padstow
Yields positive similes, apt enough
To one who dreaded these wrecking cliffs
Sixty years back but fears nothing now.

Sea-pinks and feathered singers
Distract from the ponderous breakers
Moaning or rasping at the stone ribs.

In my spinning mind,
Fresh from a bright noisy service,
Bonnets and tambourines distract
From heavy culture at all levels,
Vagabond-dark or curled coy in pulpits.

Coast road from Newquay!
There's a broad view, but for me
The petal, the warble, the girl-cadet's drum
Outlive the tides of sad wisdom.

Village Carnival

(St Stephen, August 1928)

Festooned lorries filed slowly by,
And farm-waggons drawn by puzzled horses
Wondering about the curbèd pace,
The receding swagger of a brass band,
The frisk of gaudy ribbons
Easing the hot rub of harness.
The whole cavalcade was watched by birds,
Alarmed among summer-thick trees
Behind the crowded roadside.

On each vehicle the disguised,
Performing girls and workmen swayed and jested,
Some of them singing, swinging accordions
Which panted old tunes in the twilight
While the young voices sent familiar words
Floating into the day's ebb.

Most onlookers laughed, feeling the fun of it,
But I could not laugh, I was too deeply moved,
Aware of unbearable poignancy
In the haunting song and brave, frail colour.

Moor Hunt

A dredger at that sour and shabby pool
Like a blood-sucking vampire; the flat heath
Bristling for miles, its massive threat unsoftened
By a hedged road, cottage or cordial tree.

I had known from infancy
That this was Goss Moor, but I feared the place,
Never cheered when my well-meaning uncle
Led me out past the groping dredger,
The choked tarn, to see huntsmen arrive
On an autumn afternoon, hailing from Fowey.

Brightly-clad folk on horses, urging
Lean hounds that sniffed or bayed,
Scenting prey. It seemed all of a piece
With the blood-sucking image by the pool.
I would picture the trapped fox and creep,
Hurt and shaken, back to Penrose farm,
Where a bucket soon clacked in the homely well
And I could relax, ready for the bracing tea.

Cloud Over Bugle

We know pollution in these parts:
Mica-stain thick on running water,
Stack-fumes fouling sunshine and mist,
White clay-dust clogging lawns and doormats,
Parsley-clumps, rhubarb leaves, pea-pods,
And such blackberries as find space to exist.

But this would be worse, the sinister
Elaborate spell of the nuclear chamber,
Replacing the exhausted coal, sucking us back
Into the tense war atmosphere,
Dread of poison gas, evacuation,
And the chilling fascination
Of the mute mushroom over Hiroshima.

Must we taste, besides clay, the freaks of science
In new ways of maiming the unborn,
Planting cancer through radioactive air
That rots the pit-narrowed corn, the remnant of trees?
Shall we envy our sires by their safe peat fires,
And their brides breeding in the pure breeze?

In 1980 a mid-Cornwall clay district site near Bugle was chosen for the building of a nuclear power station, but after mass demonstrations of protest the scheme was abandoned.

Wheal Martyn

That blunt unsentimental treasure-store,
Museum of the practical,
Sifts and displays a strong white history,
Two hundred years of harsh bargaining
In miners' idiom. The peaked, pronged dumps,
Noisy craters, engine-houses, sheds
Have been raked to furnish those rooms.

Tourists may smile at uncouth iron,
Or shudder as in a torture-chamber,
Till they scan the delicate products –
The lucid cup, coy vase and glossy paper.

I once explored that building,
Pressing there in grey weather,
Heart fresh from palms and sea-toned rose-clumps,
And I was confused, felt split.
That world of the man who had been me –
Was it cradle or jail, a grotesque monastery
Or image-fertile with my nuptial clay?

My forebears had swung the pick-axe,
Focused the hose-drill on diseased rock,
Set the hurricane-lantern in a safe crevice
On night shifts, stumbling in wet corduroys
Tied with string. Some had kicked powdery cubes
Beside the boiling kiln-pan, their hobnail boots
Stiff as wooden clogs with thick dry mud.
Those days come alive at Wheal Martyn,
But part of me was immune – it had moved away.

I know little of modern methods
Eloquent there too. I suppose they are cleaner,
More complex, efficient enough
To make workmen redundant,
And, lacking the raw energy
Which ignites faith through a symbol,
They lay no track or pipeline for my song.

Bridges

(for Rachelle)

Turning from Guineaport Parc
And a friend's new home, not yet furnished,
We enter twisting streets that feel ancient,
And I fancy they were here when Cromwell came.

A blaze of voice and eye, on a steaming horse
Reined on the Camel bridge, he ordered his troops
To foil a Royalist crossing... That's now a dark
Shadow of history. Here's today's rejoinder,
The splutter and flash of peace-maddened traffic
Above the river, the unguarded stone.

This town, Wadebridge, is unknown to me,
And I tread its pavements sharing neither
Cromwell's mood, drilling for mindless battle,
Nor the bright unthinking rush of a holiday crowd.

A poet in a new setting
Guards the identity which seeks a response
From outside, a link-up signal.
But the bridge can have no place in my confirmation.
Civil War tactics, the modern herd
Speeding to animal heats or decently godless –
They both miss the rhythms I listen for.

The thrill of proving a fresh scene
True to my weaned essential taste
Stirred hopefully in our friend's bare rooms, and will spread
When a grace is said at the installed table.

That's a nice irony. I was feasted
With my first contacts abroad, finding the exact aura
Of my hushed life's drama
In the silent Venetian bridges,
And the normal, unblocked ones, taking pilgrims
Across the Arno, in Tuscany's deep Florence.

Casa Guidi

(for Benedict Ramsden)

Narrow study, spacious drawing-room
Fuse in neglect, but a clinging fresco
Seems potent, cancelling the emptiness
Of the unfurnished apartments.
These pale blue walls look unperturbed,
Not robbed of essential treasure, nor drained
Of the vibrant magic that pierced me in Cornwall
With my first Browning pages, read in crisis.

I step to a window ornate but shuttered,
And imagine San Felice church
In the palace shade, where regular chanting voices
Jarred on him somewhat, yet attuned him
(Though less than Elizabeth's plumed kiss)
To the blue sky of a robust summer faith.

I'm an odd shoot amid this hollowed splendour –
A clot from among the workers, clay-toughened: yes,
But it bred no ragged Red in me.
Under the cracked slates my raw quirks tallied
With his perception of divine truth
Growing more firmly lucid through an uncouth style.

Between the church chants and the Arno
His pen was turbulent, bringing soul-quakes,
Not always aesthetic pleasure.
His tangle of key meanings, clues to God,
Led straight to the heart of my marriage.

Soon I shall stand on the balcony,
My wife's hand and mine on a roughly-carved cherub.
The same sun burnished Via Maggio
When that pair slowly paced the terrace,
Discussing Euripides or Cavour,
Or merely recalling Wimpole Street
And their life of wonders unfolding.

PART THREE

Nutshell

(for Pat, James & Cerris)

My hand, rarely uncertain,
Dives to the wrinkled leathery skins,
Lifts from a drawer two hard brown chestnuts,
Long lodged in Dorset, kept
As docile and sturdy souvenirs,
Safe from a slitting fingernail
And the teeth of the untaught.

These chestnuts had their season at Vallombrosa,
Swelling their limp shells in sub-tropical heat,
Or dripping in Tuscan rainstorms.
They were nudged by silent priests,
Noisy tourists from America,
Black-haired Florentine girls who needed neither
Hill-top church, nor nut-heavy grove
To prompt their capricious wonder.

Before my chestnuts fell, the shades of wind
That made them quiver or slap fanned lover,
Spread on the plain and stirred the Arno.
Its age of caprice was over,
The time when its silence meant
A baked naked ditch, breeding infection,
Or when the noise of burst banks and bridges
Caused hearts to quail at the swelling blight.

I gather all these images
Of Italian river and forest
As my chestnuts drop neatly back
Amid papers and a wooden foot-rule.
There's a glad gain in measuring
Our trivial trophies against the ache
Of a vast, ever-flowing maturity.

Dorchester Ward

Gale-force autumnal cuts were halted
By sturdy windows, and the healing process
Continued silently in the hot male ward,
On the well-spaced row of high beds.
Some men slumped in unnatural peace
After injections, others sat awkwardly,
Trailing distasteful tubes
That coiled to loaded metal frames.

Nothing looked normal here
Except the fresh flowers on the patients' lockers,
Bringing garden smells amid polish and chemicals.
Even the brisk, compassionate nurses
Moved withdrawn from the outside street life,
Handling steel instruments, rubber gear,
Taking blood pressure, temperature,
Pulse-rate, their minds holding figures
Cold for clinical charts.

Cells would soon mend for most of us,
Old Dorset males and me the intruder,
Surprisingly pitched among them.
I probed no man for his philosophy,
His placing or rebuttal
Of pain and fever in the loom of cosmic love.

My soul breathed a more genial air
Than that of average sufferers: I was nourished
Only by joy and the years of exemption
When no ill-wind cut to the heart. My faith
Pulled clear of plausible doubts
And honest wintry surmises. I grasped
Always the pledge of unfailing spring,
Even here with Hardy's statue forbidding.

Growing in Grace

My native clay
Symbols grow unreal.
Blunt clanging tools
Corroded rock
Kiln-scorching...
O Shepherd
Of green pastures!

Purgation's landscape
Fails to purge,
Makes us afraid.
Slap of hose-jets
Blinding
Deafening blast
Rattle on bleared dunes
Scoops' and sirens'
Howl over stagnant mud.

Waters of Meribah.
I proved thee at the...
I proved thee.
Baptised into the death...
O Shepherd
Of green pastures!

Beach Ritual

Thin tattooed arms swing up from the clean tide;
Waist-long hair of radiant back-street molls
Drips and gropes on freakish apparel;
God-tapping song floats in a rough wind, puzzling
Prim Pharisees and sullen gulls.
Here's a rare prong of baptism
Fiery amid seaweed.

These nomads are at home
On trustworthy Western sands,
Cheating the foreign siren, the slant-eyed
Fringe where faith ebbed and a sick culture
Called up the illicit dream-image.

Soaked, fully clothed, free in the new spell,
They wade to defy the stealthy pusher,
Wade back to grief or salvage among their kind –
The drifting wrecks who have dropped
On this same beach the black ritual needle.

Schooling

Trendy mists and the venerable anchor
Lying unused as she plunged or drifted
Towards a select career.
News leaked, and flakes of her verse,
From the swirling campus.
Echoes of Plath and Cummings,
New rhythms of gloom, death-wish
Or death-of-God wish, bent her taste
Away from the blithe church chorus.

The fog thickened through a year of silence:
I missed the unique pledge,
The baptised hand still playful,
Gospelling wavelengths in the light clasp
At the pew's edge
Or in the carpeted, quay-bordered aisle.
Petition in numbed suspense
Taught me nothing.

Yet a marvel closed the desolation
Of my private lesson-base:
Not as a flow from painful training
Or a solemn prize for the disciplined soul.
Fear of the mists, the drag of a faithless harbour,
Vanished amid a clatter of cups
And trivial gossip at a church tea.

I sat there, dully immune
From traps of the cultural tide;
I ate cake stolidly
Between run-of-the-mill greetings.
But sudden, incredibly different,
That touch... I was feasting
With the restored truth of her,
And the shock of the old, eternal mirth
Relit my school of prayer.

Jack London

Between Melville's time and Hemingway's
Another voice found their pitch – a slum boy's,
Trained amid cannery bobbins in San Francisco.
He felt the loud wall, the hot smear,
The sting of his child-labour's wages
And his mother's tongue. Life, barred from love and faith,
Forced an early outlet, the one shoot
Of sane, uncrippled movement in the darkness –
A cool clear art. His pen retaliated.

That pain-built trap of words
Caught with stark honesty the ghetto scum,
Lawless hobo roaming, daemon-driven sail
To seek relief in wild Pacific glamour,
And, most memorably, the frozen trauma
Of the Klondike gold rush. Hordes of dead souls,
Ice-bitten bodies, lost in yellow mirage;
Prowl and howl of wolves and madmen
Weird in Polar twilight;
Revolver shots in doomed camps
Where fires had died through blizzard avalanches.

Restrained portrayal saved London's mind
And made his fortune, but his heart stayed numb.
Slum-twist of the misbegotten,
Uncured by a faith, set the trail to a sorry end.
The rich artist preened in his mansion
Before the flames clawed it down, while the torn
Bride-bond had brought him his only offspring.
His Californian luxury ill fitted
The remnants of raw class-hatred:
There was blind defiance, smell of liquor and ashes,
Then the white silence at forty.

Foreign Idiom

Rain was still vigorous at Haworth
When, almost at December's close,
I was stung by it outside the parsonage.
The stiff tilting street remained passive
Under the thump and slither of the deluge:
There was a general air of apt weather,
A pitiless saga's true idiom.

Many pilgrims were puzzled in that museum,
Sad, shrinking from tragic relics
Which mocked the selling dream-fiction, the ecstasy
Of high unruly hopes secure on the page
In great art. Satire at the news level:
Blind Byron-twisted heats led to a death-trap,
The last feeble prayer or the throttled mutiny.

I might have mused on scholars' theories
And returned to the rain, gone home baffled.
But I arrived there counting my blessings, a rich win
Such as the parsonage dreamers never gained
(Long wedlock, suburban comforts, God ticked travel),
And these gifts were clues I must believe in.

Cornish blood, a crude hill-crest village,
Fierce stunted moors – these features marked the Brontës
And moulded me, but the parallel broke abruptly.
I was starved and storm-warped, feeling exiled,
Then sailed out into sunshine, spoke the language
Not of Haworth but Casa Guidi,
And there's no point in asking why.

Fitting In

A heave of the car and I was across the Camel
In a gaunt Cornish autumn, heralding shrill moors;
Then, in a day or two, the real lift, landing at Pisa,
And soon I stepped bemused
Above an incredibly different river.

Nothing gaunt there: hot sunshine relaxed us
At an open-air table in the Square
Where Michelangelo's probing nude of David
Had ceased to shock British tourists.

Fingering a medieval stone buttress,
I felt myself a native of both worlds,
Cornish bleakness and Latin charm,
With private keynotes not bred by either.

The Camel was wryly native to me
In its practical push amid bare cottages,
Farm and fishery skills and the bustle of tradesmen.
I knew these levels, but the hunger for art spurred me more:
Pin-points of truth made visual
In my type of skill, creative through my wholeness only.

I still ate English food in Florence;
I brought back works of Tuscan craftsmen
To adorn my English lounge:
There is interchange and balance:
Neither by the Camel nor the Arno am I split.

T. E. Lawrence

Just here, in this crabbed Dorset hut,
    Lawrence, you pieced an Arabian saga, heights
Of valour and endurance, but
    Never the sound hearth's comforts, bridal rights.

You loved red barren sand,
    Detesting marriage and St Paul:
Even at your door I cannot understand
    Such a creature's world at all.

I thrive on Pauline toughness, grace at home
    In awkward signatures of bliss
When seven or more pillars of crusty wisdom
    Crash as a creed transforms a kiss.

There was, of course, the fact
    That your birth was illegitimate.
This must be said with tact:
    It was, in your day, unfortunate.

You screened the bruise of shame,
    Clutched at a harsh material sanctity
Of drilled machines, war flame
    And danger's dubious mystery.

Did hints of a broad transcendence
    Strike as your motor-cycle roared
To the fatal thud? Perhaps the essence
    Of our debt to you lies stored

In the track of Homer, your Odyssey,
    The tremulous Greek hope
Set in a new candour. Still, this house is empty,
    Voiceless to me. I have no taste for a grope.

Milton Abbey

We tread snappish gravel, baked turf,
Down from the stifling car, the petrol taint,
Dust-belch, wrangle of heatwave traffic.
We are thirsty – not for a quaint
Medieval ruin, each bony wall
Hammered by pitiless sun-drill,
But for the intact, peace-yielding shadow,
Cool ancient hall and cloister
Still breathing the nurture of triumphant music.

Will it be slender madrigal
Or massive anthem that sends the next echo
Soaring among those arches? Centuries
Of dedicated voices have sealed this place
From common discords – war, slave-labour,
Learning turned sour, the highwayman's curt pistol.
Here Fielding, on his turbulent rambles,
May have paused to listen – perhaps, like us
Thirsting for a fresher culture
Than he could sense when, dreaming on Bulbarrow,
He linked it with old Parnassus.

Corfe and Poole

Near the base of the scorched forbidding slope
Our Landrover quivered like a baffled tank,
At a standstill while curious eyes
Peered through its windows at the reserved shell
Of Corfe Castle. We could all imagine
The intact hill-seat, armour and banquets,
Fort walls guarding a noble tradition,
Making the shepherds, cobblers, reddlemen
Feel safer in their low hamlets.

The track was too steep for our vehicle:
We lumbered away from the high roots,
Our schoolgirls thinking of courtly splendour,
Peacocks, falcons and tapestries,
And my wife's mind turning, as we rocked towards Poole,
To more private roots – her father's childhood
On that coastal strip before his guard failed
And the enchanted castle fell.

In an hour or two the town nudged us:
We trudged to the shore, climbed a soft bank
Of pale drifted sand. New fancies stirred.
Quills of the coarse beach-grass
Might be shrill and frozen in winter gales
Like the Corfe ruins – a whole clump bent,
Scraping helplessly, although still safe
From the reined invading tide.
But ours was a summer viewpoint, the caress
Of friendly reeds whose unstrained fibres
Fed in the sand her father trusted.
A trusting heart receives its change of season,
And she glowed within the parable.

Heard at Sandsfoot

Narrow boards, three tiers, rid of sand-clots left by shoes,
Rotten planks replaced, brambles cut back
Where they had dangled, scratching hands on the rail:
The beach-steps look merry and vibrate
With a quick drum of feet. A rainbow range
Of summer dresses flits up and down
From tide-level to bush-buttoned cliff-top.

An overturned boat sprawls on the shingle,
Sandcastles are pushed flat by gentle waves;
But I do not think of wreck and demolition,
Though the fog-signal bleats on Portland Bill –
A remote discord, speaking of coast peril.

The mist is not here at Sandsfoot yet,
But I know that vibration, so different
From the bounce of bathed bodies on this beach exit.
I have felt, close up, the first thundering shock
Shake the ground like a bomb-drop
Before Pulpit Rock got its point rubbed out
By a smothering mask of sea-vapour.

Visitors' dogs were frightened, some children screamed,
Others laughed, enjoying the deafening bark
Which injured no one. I fancy the headland now
As I pat the sleeping boat.

Warfare against ill-weather, meaning
Safety for ships. On decks out at sea
Sailors are sealed in an uncanny ghost-glide,
Denied a glimpse of cliffs or lighthouse,
But trusting the rhythmic roar on the dry tongue.

Morning Call

The media had shown us an eclipse,
And I thought of Volga boats, then ventured nearer
The Arno ones. Time's habit spilled again
In a sunny glimpse on an autumn morning.

Stubbornly non-political in England,
I had never breathed in a tent or hall
While a statesman of any brand breathed the same air.
It happened in Venice, in St Mark's Cathedral,
Of all places where life's ironies
Can add to a holiday smile.

A crowd jostled outside, teased by chaotic doves,
And eager to cheer the Moscow visitor
Who had striven to lift his people from a cold nightmare,
Soul-drained steppes, dead-eyed robot cities,
Into a morning of free speech and action.

I sat quietly, resting tired feet
While candles and altar-carvings vied –
The twinkle, the heavy sanctity –
To impress tough fibre long galled in irreligion.

Was my faith's fibre more at home there?
Would Bunyan have felt closer to St Mark's
Than Lenin? I'm classed as heretic,
But both these men reflect past climates,
And the Russian leader who was being shown
The Church's wealth, became conditioned,
As I did, by a broader concept
Of unity, transcending
A personal taste, party line or iron curtain.

Mikhail Gorbachev visited St Mark's Cathedral, Venice,
on 20th September 1993.

Heretic in Florence

A clouding glory sprouted here
In Tuscan sunshine. This is not Geneva,
Where broken spirits took the divine graft
Clear of Churchdom, Papal patronage of art,
Soiled motives of the maker. I'm a poet
Of Calvin's trend, one of the sparse tribe
From English Dissent who found this relaxed city,
This soft fount of culture, a strange, split home.
Milton came first, and then, at Casa Guidi,
The Brownings fused aesthete and Puritan.

Creative minds may trespass, leave the soul
Dry as the Arno bed that gaped each summer
Before Dante's day and even while da Vinci
Plotted to cure the unruly river
Which gushed, flagged, whimpered, turned to cadaverous mud –
As art does when proudly scorning
Heaven's grace, Church-tracked or elemental.

I face the worst records, my tastes undaunted.
There were Florentine monks, young profligates,
Who showed the Virgin chaste on canvas
And hated rival painters who got more pay.
There were weaklings, swindlers like del Sarto,
Serving the Holy See, correct in technique,
Never inspired, drained by their pagan wives.
I was awed by towering Michaelangelo
On his abnormal verge. I shrank from Dante
As he barred his wife out, let the idol phantom
Guide him to a classic paradise.

How far can God's grace move the beholder
Of mere cold skill or twisted vision?
I sense the fringe, an electing flow.
Summer heat has sucked churches, galleries
And the river bridge I stand on,
But there's no whimpering trickle, no silent bed:
The cured Arno sings in freedom.